STORMY TIMES, THRIVING AFTER LOSS

Feeding Mind Soul and Body

Carmen Anderson-Harris

New American Standard Bible (NASB)
New American Standard Bible®, Copyright © 1960, 1971, 1977, 1995, 2020 by The Lockman Foundation. All rights reserved.
New International Version (NIV)
Holy Bible, New International Version®, NIV® Copyright ©1973, 1978, 1984, 2011 by Biblica, Inc.® Used by permission. All rights reserved worldwide.

Scripture taken from the King James Version of the Bible.
New American Standard Bible 1995 (NASB1995)
New American Standard Bible®, Copyright © 1960, 1971, 1977, 1995 by The Lockman Foundation. All rights reserved.
New King James Version (NKJV)
Scripture taken from the New King James Version®. Copyright © 1982 by Thomas Nelson. Used by permission. All rights reserved.
New American Standard Bible 1997 (NASB1997)
New American Standard Bible Copyright © 1960, 1962, 1963, 1968, 1971, 1972, 1973, 1975, 1977, 1995 by The Lockman Foundation, La Habra, Calif. All rights reserved.

To order additional copies of this book, contact:
Xlibris
844-714-8691
www.Xlibris.com
Orders@Xlibris.com

ISBN: Softcover   978-1-6641-9141-9
         EBook   978-1-6641-9142-6

Print information available on the last page

Rev. date: 08/23/2021

Feeding our body and our Spirit is a must for all the seasons of life, no matter our age or status. God expects ALL of His children to nourish our spirit and soul.

Only the individual can do this.... We have to 'feed ourselves' on purpose.

The past twenty years, God and His Holy Spirit, has used these Scriptures portions to comfort soothe, and replenished me during a time of sorrow, testing and trials and even the questions I have had at times during this special journey.

These words of comfort have brought healing, and have been the guard at the door of my mind and thoughts and have kept the intruder (Satan) out.

The Word of God is like a pillow that we can find warm and inviting, reliable, comforting, filled with promises, that will bring great assurances that we can rely on in whatever the season of our life.

I am sharing some of these precious verses with you from my 'Basket of Blessings'. I pray that these nourishing Scriptures, Poems and pictures will help you feel comforted, your joy restored and your strength rekindled by our Lord the Great Physician who helps us to thrive after any storms.

DEDICATED TO

My friends, church family, mothers, fathers, children, daughter Renee' and my son Nathan and especially my friend Yvonne who has walked this path of sorrows and is now thriving. Yvonne, has been a Grief Share Teacher as she uses her victorious life helping those who mourn, to find strength and peace.

To all who have, and are embracing life even when we are facing losses and storms of all kinds, please remember this truth, found in Scriptures, Matthew chapter 5:4 (NIV)-

"Blessed are those who mourn, for they shall be comforted", We will be comforted by the One Who is always ready to step in our discomforts and trials just as He did for Mary and her sister Martha, at the loss of their brother Lazarus.

Please allow Him to help you pick up the pieces of your life and steady your feet as you thrive and bless others knowing that flowers blooms after a long Winter and so will you and I.

ACKNOWLEDGMENTS

To all my friends who have tasted some of the joys and sorrows of this life, I pray that you will Pick up the pieces of your life and with God's help to thrive and be a comfort to others who will walk this road some day.

Feeding our mind, soul and body, has to be intentional and I do hope you will as I have done. God does not do the thriving for us, but He does give courage, comfort and strength to keep moving forward. Don't be a parked car, but let God help you steer through life with joy.

A New Year Dawns

A new year is dawning
With many hearts a churning
Wondering how to face the new year
Will it be mourning, joy or disappear?

There is hope in the new year
God and His heavenly host is near,
To be the guide and help you need
So lift your heart in prayerful plead

Oh Father of all mercies
Forgive our foolishness and follies.
We regret the course we have taken
Against your will, we were mistaken

Forgive us Lord we deserve your wrath
We plead for grace as we walk the path
We humble our hearts before you dear Father,
Your love touches us more than any other.

Give unto the Lord, The glory due to His name
Worship the Lord in the beauty of holiness
Psalm 29:2 (KJV)

Basket of Blessings Verses

"Be anxious for nothing, but in everything by prayer and supplication, with thanksgiving, let your requests be made known to God". Philippians 4:6 (NASB)

"Jesus Christ is the same yesterday and today and forever. Through Him then, let us continually offer up a sacrifice of praise to God, that is, the fruit of lips that give thanks to His name'. Hebrews 13:8,15 (NASB1995)

"But let all who take refuge in Thee be glad, let them ever sing for joy, and mayest Thou shelter them, that those who love Thy name may exult in Thee" Psalm 5:11 (NASB1995)

Jesus said to them, " I am the bread of life, he who comes to me, shall not hunger and he who believes in Me, shall never thirst". John 6:35 (NASB)

"I called out of my distress to the Lord, and He answered me. I cried for help from the depth of Sheol, Thou didst hear my voice". Jonah 2:2 (NASB)

"Come let us return to the Lord, For He has torn us, but He will heal us

He has wounded us, but He will bandage us". Hosea 6:1 (NASB)

"If then God so arrays the the grass, which isalive today and tomorrow is thrown into the oven; how much more will he clothe you, O men of little faith". Luke 12:28 (NASB)

"Pleasant words are a honeycomb, sweet to the soul and healing to the bones". Proverbs 16:24 (NASB)

"But after you have suffered for a little while, the God of all grace, who called you to His eternal glory in Christ, will Himself perfect, confirm, strengthen and establish you. To Him be dominion forever and ever, Amen!" 1 Peter 5:10-11 (NASB)

Then said Jesus to those Jews which believed on Him, " If you abide in My word, Then you are truly disciples of mine. And you shall know the truth and the truth shall make you free". John 8:31-32 (NKJV)

"Salt is good, but if the salt becomes unsalty with what will you make it salty again? Have salt in yourselves, and be at peace with one another". Mark 9:50 (NASB)

"I remember the days of old, I meditate on all thy doings; I muse on the work of Your hands. I stretch out my hands to Thee; My soul longs for Thee as a parched land". Psalm 143:5-6 (KJV)

"Give ear to my words, O Lord, consider my groaning Heed the sound of my cries for help my King and my God, for to Thee do I pray. In the morning O Lord thou wilt hear my voice; In the morning I will order my prayer to Thee and eagerly watch". Psalm 5:1-3 (NASB1995)

"Go therefore and make disciples of all nations, baptizing them in the name of the Father and of the Son and of the Holy Spirit". Matthew 28:19 (NASB)

Teaching them to observe all things whatsoever I command you; and lo, I am with you always, even unto the end of the world". Matthew 28:20 (KJV)

"I love the O Lord my strength. The Lord is my rock and my fortress and my deliverer. My God, my rock, in whom I take refuge. My shield and the horn of my salvation, my stronghold. I call upon the Lord Who is worthy to be praised and I am saved from my enemies". Psalm 18:1-3 (NASB1995)

"The Lord is in your midst, a victorious warrior He will exult over you with joy. He will be quiet in His love. He will rejoice over you with shouts of joy". Zephaniah 3:17 (NASB1995)

"Ask and it shall be given to you; seek and you shall find; knock and it shall be opened to you. For everyone who asks receives, and he who seeks finds and to him who knocks it shall be opened". Matthew 7:7-8 (NASB1997)

"Now Jabez called on the God of Israel saying," O that thou wouldst bless me indeed, and enlarge my border and that Thy hand might be with me, and that wouldst keep me from harm that it may not pain me"! And God granted him what he requested". 1 Chronicles 4:10 (NASB1997)

"Let us therefore draw near with confidence to the throne of grace, that we may receive mercy and may find grace to help in time of need". Hebrews 4:16 (NASB1997)

"And without faith it is impossible to please Him, for he who comes to God must believe that He is, and that He is a rewarder of those who diligently seek Him". Hebrews 11:6 (NKJV)

"Let us not lose heart in doing good, for in due time we shall reap if we do not grow weary. So then, while we have opportunity, let us do good to all men, and especially to those who are of the household of the faith". Galatians 6:9-10 (NASB1997)

"But thanks be to God who gives us the victory through our Lord Jesus Christ.

Therefore my beloved brethren, be steadfast, immovable, always abounding in the work of the Lord, knowing that your toil is not in vain in the Lord". 1 Corinthians 15:57-58 (NASB1995)

He sends His sunshine and rain on everyone
We know He'll always hold our hands.
God has so many ways to teach me today,
About His marvelous creation.

"And whatever we ask we receive from Him, because we keep His commandments and do the things that are pleasing in His sight". 1 John 3:22 (NASB)

"Blessed are those who mourn, for they shall be comforted. Blessed are those who hunger and thirst for righteousness, for they shall be satisfied". Matthew 5:4; 6 (NASB1995)

"Therefore I say to you, all things for which you pray and ask, believe that you have received them, and they shall be granted you. And whenever you stand praying, forgive. If you have anything against anyone, so that your Father also who is in heaven, may forgive you your transgressions". Mark 11:24-25 (NASB1997)

"Do not fear O land, rejoice and be glad for the Lord has done great things. Do not fear beasts of the field, for the pastures of the wilderness have turned green, for the trees have borne it's fruit. The fig tree and the vine have yielded in full". Joel 2:21-22 (NASB1995)

"O Lord thou art my God, I will exalt thee, I will give thanks to Thy name, for thou hast worked wonders, plans formed long ago, with perfect faithfulness". Isaiah 25:1 (NASB1997)

"The steadfast of mind Thou wilt keep in perfect peace, because he trust in Thee. Trust in the Lord forever, for in God the Lord, we have an everlasting rock". Isaiah 26:3-4 (NASB1997)

"I will lift up my eyes to the mountains, from whence shall my help comes; My help comes from the Lord who made heaven and earth. He will not allow your foot to slip; He who keeps you will not slumber, behold He Who keeps Israel will neither slumber nor sleep". Psalm 121:1-4 (NASB1997)

"Now to Him who is able to do exceeding abundantly beyond all that we ask or think, according to the power that works within us, to Him be glory in the church and in Christ Jesus to all generations forever and ever, Amen". Ephesians 3:20-21 (NASB1997)

"The words of the mouth of a wise man are gracious, but the lips of a fool consume him". Ecclesiastes 10:12 (NASB1995)

"God is our refuge and strength, a very present help in trouble. Therefore we will not fear, though the earth should change and though the mountain slip into the heart of the sea". Psalm 46:1-2 (NASB1995)

"The Lord is good, a stronghold in the day of trouble, and He knows those who take refuge in Him. But with an overflowing flood, He will make a complete end of its site and will pursue His enemies into darkness". Nahum 1:7-8 (NASB1995)

"Sing to the Lord a new song; sing to the Lord all the earth. Sing to the Lord, bless His name; Proclaim good tidings of His salvation from day to day". Psalm 96:1-2 (NASB1995)

"How lovely on the mountains are the feet of him who brings good news of happiness, who announces salvation and says to zion, Your God reigns". Isaiah 52:7 (NASB)

"God is not a man that He should lie, nor a son of man, that He should repent. Has He said and will He not do it? Or has He spoken, and will He not make it good?" Numbers 23:19 (NASB1995)

"Let us hold fast the confession of our hope without wavering, for He who promised is faithful". Hebrews 10:23 (NASB1995)

You are my inspiration and satisfaction
You are my lover, confidant and admiration
You are my fair, ruddy partner before creation
You satisfy and beautify, you're my soul's adoration.

"Consider it all joy my brethren when you encounter various trials, knowing that the testing of your faith produces endurance". James 1:2-3 (NASB1995)

"In order that by two unchangeable things in which it is impossible for God to lie. We may have strong encouragement we who have fled for refuge in laying hold of the hope set before us. This hope we have as an anchor of the soul, a hope both sure and steadfast and one which enters within the veil". Hebrews 6:18-19 (NASB1997)

"My soul wait in silence for God only for my hope is from Him. He only is my rock and my salvation, my stronghold, I shall not be shaken". Psalm 62:5-6 (NASB1995)

"Shout joyfully to the Lord all the earth, break forth and sing for joy and sing praises". Psalm 98:4 (NASB1995)

"Not one of the good promises which the Lord had made to the house of Israel failed; all came to pass". Joshua 21:45 (NASB1995)

HIS LOVE IS EVERLASTING

Tell the world about His love
It's sent down from heaven above
His love so pure so sweet so true
It is safe, it cures when you are blue

God's love is everywhere
You feel Him for His love is near
Things change because his love renew
Embrace it, trust it He's a friend so true

His love is seen in every flower,
In every rain and stormy shower
His love is seen in a beautiful butterfly
Let your spirit soar like fireflies

His sweet pure love in a rainbow
His gentle love piles up row by row
Oh, let your heart soar up high
God's love will lift you above the sky

"Do you not know? Have you not heard? The Everlasting God, the Lord, the Creator of the ends of the earth does not become weary or tired. His understanding is inscrutable. He gives strength to the weary, and to him who lacks might, He increases power". Isaiah 40:28-29 (NASB1995)

"Guard my soul and deliver me, do not let me be ashamed for I take refuge in Thee. Let integrity and uprightness preserve me, for I wait for Thee". Psalm 25:20-21 (NASB1997)

"Humble yourselves, therefore, under the mighty hand of God, that He may exalt you at the proper time. Casting your anxiety upon Him, because He cares for you". 1 Peter 5:6-7 (NASB1997)

"And this is the confidence which we have before Him that, if we ask anything according to His will, He hears us. And if we know that He hears us in whatever we ask, we know that we have the requests which we have asked from Him". 1 John 5:14-15 (NASB1997)

"Now to Him Who is able to keep you from stumbling and to make you stand in the presence of His glory blameless with great joy, to the only God our Savior, through Jesus Christ our Lord, be glory, majesty dominion and authority, before all time and now and forever, Amen". Jude 1:24-25 (NASB1995)

"Beloved, if our heart does not condemn us, we have confidence before God, and whatever we ask we receive from Him, because we keep His commandments and do the things that are pleasing in His sight". 1John 3:21-22 (NASB1995)

"And God is able to make all grace abound to you, that always having all sufficiency in everything, you may have an abundance for every good deed". 2 Corinthians 9:8 (NASB1997)

"How blessed is everyone who fears the Lord, who walks in His ways, when you shall eat of the fruit of your hands, you will be happy and it will be well with you". Psalm 128:1-2 (NASB1995)

"The Lord sustains all who fall and raises up all who are bowed down. The eyes of all look to Thee and Thou dost give them their food in due time. Thou dost open Thy hand and dost satisfy the desire of every living thing". Psalm 145:14-16 (NASB1997)

"I can do all things through Christ who strengthens me". Philippians 4:13 (NKJV)

"You did not choose me, but I chose you and appointed you that you should go and bear fruit, and that your fruit remain, and whatever you ask of the Father in My name, He may give you". John 15:16 (NASB1997)

"Do not fear, for I am with you; Do not anxiously look about you for I am your God. I will strengthen you, surely I will help you, surely I will uphold you with My righteous right hand". Isaiah 41:10 (NASB1995)

"Do not tremble and do not be afraid; Have I not long since announced it to you and declared it? And you are MY witnesses. Is there any God besides Me, or is there any other Rock? I know of none". Isaiah 44:8 (NASB)

"Beloved, I pray that in all respects you may prosper and be in good health, just as your soul prospers". 3 John 1:2 (NASB)

Be of good courage, and He shall strengthen
Your heart, All you who hope in the Lord
Psalm 31:24 (NKJV)

THE STRANGER BECAME A FRIEND

I met a special stranger
He was so kind and sweet
Each day our paths crossed,
He held a special place in my heart

The stranger became a friend,
O, the wonder of such a blend,
I pray, dear Lord, help us, lead us
May this friendship never ends

It seems like God Himself was near
As this friend and I became a pair;
Sharing dreams of past and present,
Keeps the joys of conversions pleasant

Sometimes it takes a lifetime,
To find a friend kind and true
Strong, yet gentle, caring, never blue
He brings happiness and understanding too

I wish you could meet my friend Ken,
On him I can always depend
God in His wisdom, power and love,
Sent me this special friend from above.

"Through Him then, let us continually offer up a sacrifice of praise to God, that is the fruit of lips that give thanks to His name. And do not neglect doing good and sharing; for with such sacrifices God is pleased". Hebrews 13:15-16 (NASB1995)

"Speaking to one another in psalms and hymns and spiritual songs, singing and making melody with your heart to the Lord. Always giving thanks for all things in the name of our Lord Jesus Christ to God even the Father". Ephesians 5:19-20 (NASB1995)

"Be strong and courageous, do not be afraid or tremble at them, for the Lord your God is the one who goes with you. He will not fail you or forsake you". Deuteronomy 31:6 (NASB1995)

"Blessed be the Lord God, the God of Israel Who alone works wonders. And blessed be His glorious name forever. And may the whole earth be filled with His glory, Amen and Amen". Psalm 72:18-19 (NASB1995)

"Thou alone art the Lord, Thou hast made the heavens, the heaven with all their host. The earth and all that is on it. The seas and all that is in them and the heavenly host bows down before Thee". Nehemiah 9:6 (NASB1997)

"But I am afflicted and in pain; May Thy salvation, O God, set me securely on high. I will praise The name of God with song and shall magnify Him with thanksgiving". Psalm 69:29-30 (NASB1997)

"Let all who seek Thee rejoice and be glad in Thee; and let those who love Thy salvation say continually, let God be magnified. But I am afflicted and needy, hasten to me O God; Thou art my help and my deliverer. O Lord do not delay". Psalm 70:4-5 (NASB1997)

"Again I say to you, that if two of you agree on earth about anything that they may ask, it shall be done for them by my Father who is in heaven. For where two or three have gathered together in My name, there I am in their midst". Matthew 18:19-20 (NASB1995)

"Do not lay up for yourselves treasures upon earth, where moth and rust destroy, and where thieves break in and steal. But lay up for yourselves treasures in heaven, where neither moth nor rust destroys, and where thieves do not break in or steal; for where your treasure is, there will your heart be also". Matthew 6:19-21 (NASB1997)

"And he will be like a tree firmly planted by streams of water, which yields its fruit in its season, and its leaf does not wither, and in whatever he does, he prospers. Psalm 1:3 (NASB1995)

"Our soul waiteth for the Lord He is our help and our shield. For our heart shall rejoice in him, because we have trusted in his holy name". Psalm 33:20-21 (KJV)

"And they sang the song of Moses the bond servant of God and the song of the Lamb, saying, Great and marvelous are Thy works, O Lord God the Almighty, Righteous and true are Thy ways, Thou King of the nations, who will not fear, and glorify Thy name? For Thou alone art holy; For all the nations will come and worship before Thee, for Thy righteous acts have been revealed". Revelation 15:3-4 (NASB1997)

"I will feed My flock and I will lead them to rest, declares the Lord God. I will seek the lost, bring back the scattered, bind up the broken, and strengthen the sick, but the fat and the strong I will destroy. I will feed them with judgment". Ezekiel 34:15-16 (NASB1995)

"For God hath not given us the spirit of fear, but of power and love and of a sound mind" 2 Timothy 1:7 (KJV)

"And the Lord will continually guide you and satisfy your desire in scorched places, and give strength to your bones, and you will be like a watered garden and like a spring of water whose waters do not fail". Isaiah 58:11 (NASB)

"Hear me O Lord for Thy lovingkindness is good; turn unto me according to the multitude of thy tender mercies and hide not they face from thy servant; for I am in trouble, hear me speedily". Psalm 69:16-17 (KJV)

Commit your works to the Lord;
And your thoughts will be established
Proverbs 16:3 (NKJV)

"Therefore we do not lose heart, but though our outer man is decaying, yet our inner man is being renewed day by day" 2 Corinthians 4:16 (NASB1995)

"He makes me lie down in green pastures; He leads me beside quiet waters. He restores my soul, He guides me in the paths of righteousness for His name's sake." Psalm 23:2-3 (NASB1995)

"How sweet are thy words to my taste! Yes, sweeter than honey to my mouth. Thy word is a lamp to my feet, and a light to my path". Psalm 119:103, 105 (NASB1997)

"The Lord's loving-kindness indeed never cease, for His compassion never fail they are new every morning; great is Thy faithfulness. The Lord is my portion, says my soul, therefore I have hope in Him. The Lord is good to those who wait for Him, to the person who seeks Him". Lamentations 3:22-25 (NASB1997)

"Come unto me, all who are weary and heavy-laden, and I will give you rest. Take my yoke upon you, and learn from me, for I am gentle and humble in heart, and you shall find rest for your souls, for my yoke is easy and my load is light". Matthew 11:28-30 (NASB1997)

"However, you are not in the flesh but in the Spirit, if indeed the Spirit of God dwells in you. But if anyone does not have the Spirit of Christ, he does not belong to Him". Romans 8:9 (NASB)

"But in all these things we overwhelmingly conquer through Him who loved us. For I am convinced that neither death nor life, nor angels, nor principalities, nor things present, nor things to come, nor powers, nor heights, nor depth nor any other created thing, shall be able to separate us from the love of God, which is in Christ Jesus our Lord". Romans 8:37-39 (NASB1995)

"This book of the law shall not depart from your mouth, but you shall meditate on it day and night, so that you may be careful to do according to all that is written in it, for then you will make your way prosperous, and then you will have success". Joshua 1:8 (NASB1995)

"For I know the plans that I have for you, declares the Lord, Plans for welfare and not for calamity to give you a future and a hope. Then you will call upon me and come and pray to me, and I will listen to you. And you will seek me and find me, when you search for me with all your heart". Jeremiah 29:11-13 (NASB1995)

"This poor man cried and the Lord heard him and saved him out of all his troubles. The angel of the Lord encamps around those who fear Him, and rescues them". Psalm 34:6-7 (NASB1995)

"In Thee O Lord I have taken refuge, let me never be ashamed. In Thy righteousness deliver me. Incline Thine ear to me quickly, be thou to me a rock of strength, a stronghold to save me for Thou art my rock and my fortress for Thy name's sake, Thou wilt lead me and guide me". Psalm 31:1-3 (NASB1997)

"How precious is Thy lovingkindness O God, and the children of men take refuge in the shadow of Thy wings". Psalm 36:7 (NASB1997)

"I waited patiently for the Lord, and He inclined to me and heard my cry. And He put a new song in my mouth, a song of praise to our God. Many will see and fear and will trust in the Lord. How blessed is the man who has made the Lord his trust and has not turned to the proud, nor to those who lapse into falsehood". Psalm 40:1, 3-4 (NASB1997)

"Let heaven and earth praise Him. The seas and everything that moveth therein". Psalm 69:34 (KJV)

"Behold I stand at the door and knock; if anyone hears My voice and opens the door, I will come into him, and will dine with him and he with Me. He who overcomes, I will grant to him to sit down with Me on My throne, as I also overcame and sat down with My Father on His throne". Revelation 3:20-21 (NASB1995)

"On the day I called Thou didst answered me. Thou didst make me bold with strength in my soul. All the kings of the earth will give thanks to Thee, O Lord, when they have heard the words of Thy mouth, and they will sing of the ways of the Lord, for great is the glory of the Lord". Psalm 138:3-5 (NASB1997)

"Thou hast also given me the shield of Thy salvation, and Thy right hand upholds me, and Thy gentleness makes me great. Thou dost enlarge my steps under me, and my feet have not slipped". Psalm 18:35-36 (NASB1997)

"For Thou didst form my inward part; Thou didst weave me in my mother's womb. How precious also are thy thoughts to me, O God; how vast is the sum of them! If I should count them, they would out-number the sand, when I awake I am still with Thee.

Search me O God and know my heart; try me and know my anxious thoughts; and see if there be any hurtful way in me, and lead me in the everlasting way". Psalm 139:13, 17-18; 23-24 (NASB1997)

"Hide Thy face from my sins and blot out all my iniquities. Create in me a clean heart O God, and renew a steadfast spirit within me". Psalm 51:9-10 (NASB1997)

Time Marches On

Birthday celebration comes each year
With friends and family I love so dear
Their good wishes, smiles and love
Makes my heart glad as the dew from above

Years are passing from birth to now,
Oh my, I ask the reason why and how
Lord I need your strength your courage too,
To live my life as you take me through.

Rejoice for a year that is past
Rejoice for a new one is now cast,
By the God the Father who always care
Celebrate, joy, hope, and future rare

7/11/2020

"As for the terror of you, the arrogance of your heart has deceived you. O you who live in the clefts of the rock, who occupy the height of the hill, though you make your nest as high as an eagle's, I will bring you down from there, declares the Lord". Jeremiah 49:16 (NASB1995)

"The Lord God is my strength and He has made my feet like hinds' feet and makes me walk on my high places". Habakkuk 3:19 (NASB1995)

"In the day it will be said to Jerusalem; Do not be afraid O Zion; Do not let your hands fall limp. The Lord your God is in your midst, a victorious warrior, He will exult over you with joy He will be quiet in His love, He will rejoice over you with shouts of joy". Zephaniah 3:16-17 (NASB1995)

"Lord Thou hast been our dwelling place in all generations. Before the mountains were born, or thou didst

give birth the world, even from everlasting to everlasting Thou are God". Psalm 90:1-2 (NASB1997)

"Rest in the Lord and wait patiently for Him; do not fret because of him who prospers in his way, because of the man who carries out wicked schemes". Psalm 37:7 (NASB1995)

"I have come as light into the world, that everyone who believes in Me may not remain in darkness" John 12:46 (NASB1995)

"Pleasant words are a honeycomb, sweet to the soul and healing to the bones". Proverbs 16:24 (NASB 1995)

"My son, if your heart is wise, my own heart also will be glad and my inmost being will rejoice, when your lips speak what is right". Proverbs 23:15-16 (NASB1995)

"Enter His gates with thanksgiving, and His court with praise. Give thanks to Him, bless His name for the Lord is good, His lovingkindness is everlasting and His faithfulness to all generations". Psalm 100:4-5 (NASB1995)

"My beloved responded and said to me, 'Arise my darling, my beautiful one, and come along, for behold the winter is past, the rain is over and gone. The flowers have already appeared in the land; the time has arrived for pruning the vines and the voice of the turtledove has been heard in our land. The fig tree has ripened its figs, and the vines in blossom have given forth their fragrance' Arise my darling, my beautiful one, and come along". Song Of Solomon 2:10-13 (NASB1995)

"Come my beloved, let us go out into the country, let us spend the night in the villages, let us rise early and go to the vineyards let us see whether the vine has budded and its blossoms have opened, and whether the pomegranates have bloomed, there I will give you my love". Song of Solomon 7:11-12 (NASB1995)

"Though youths grow weary and tired, and vigorous young men stumble badly, yet those who wait for the Lord will gain new strength; they will mount up with wings like eagles, they will run and not get tired, they will walk and not become weary". Isaiah 40:30-31 (NASB1995)

"He will call upon me, and I will answer him; I will be with him in trouble; I will rescue him and honor him, with a long life I will satisfy him and let him behold my salvation". Psalm 91:15-16 (NASB1997)

"For Thou art great and doest wondrous deeds; Thou alone art God. Teach me Thy way O Lord. I will walk in Thy truth. Unite my heart to fear Thy name. I will give thanks to Thee, O Lord my God, with all my heart and will glorify Thy name forever". Psalm 86:10-12 (NASB1997)

But just as it is written, " Things which eye has not seen and ear has not heard and which have not entered the heart of man, all that God has prepared for those who love Him". 1 Corinthians 2:9 (NASB1995)

"Behold, I am coming quickly and My reward is with Me, to render to every man according to what he has done. I am the Alpha and the Omega, the first and the last, the beginning and the end. Blessed are those who wash their robes, that they may have the right to the tree of life, and may enter by the gates into the city". Revelation 22:13-14 (NASB1995)

"The Lord shall preserve thee from all evil; he shall preserve thy soul. The Lord shall preserve thy going out and thy coming in from this time forth, and even forever". Psalm 121:7-8 (KJV)

"Out of the depths have I cried unto thee O Lord. Lord, hear my voice; let thine ears be attentive to the voice of my supplications. If thou Lord, shouldest mark iniquities, O Lord who shall stand? But there is forgiveness with thee, that thou mayest be feared. I wait for the Lord, my soul doth wait, and in his word do I hope. My soul waiteth for the Lord, more than they that watch for the morning". Psalm 130:1-6 (KJV)

"Our soul is escaped as a bird out of the snare of the fowlers; the snare is broken and we are escaped. Our help is in the name of the Lord, who made heaven and earth". Psalm 124:7-8 (KJV)

"When thou liest down thou shalt not be afraid. Yea, thou shalt lie down, and thy sleep shall be sweet. Be not afraid of sudden fear, neither of the desolation of the wicked, when it cometh. For the Lord shall be thy confidence, and shall keep thy foot from being taken. Withhold not good from them to whom it is due, when it is in the power of thine hand to do it". Proverbs 3:24-27 (KJV)

How lovely on the mountains are the feet of him who brings good news, Who announces peace; and brings good news of happiness, who announces salvation, and says to zion, "your God reigns". Isaiah 52:7 (NASB1995)

Long before the day I met you
My life was slipping fast away,
I had no hope, I had no dream
Until your smile made my day.

"When you passest through the waters, I will be with thee; and through the rivers, They shall not overflow thee; when thou walkest through the fire, thou shall not be burned; neither shall the flame kindle upon thee. Ye are my witness saith the Lord, and my servant whom I have chosen, that you may know and believe me, and understand that I am he; before me there was no God formed, neither shall there be after me. I, even I,

I am the Lord and beside me there is no Savior". Isaiah 43:2, 10-11 (KJV)

"Every day will I bless thee, and I will praise thy name forever and ever. Great is the Lord, and greatly to be praised and his greatness is unsearchable. One generation shall praise thy works to another, and shall declare thy mighty acts. I will speak of the glorious honor of thy majesty and of thy wondrous works" Psalm 145:2-5 (KJV)

"He healeth the broken in heart, and bindeth up their wounds. He telleth the number of the stars he calleth them all by their names. Great is our Lord, and of great power; His understanding is infinite. The Lord lifteth up the meek; he casteth the wicked down to the ground. Sing unto the Lord with thanksgiving, sing praise upon the harp unto our God". Psalm 147:3-7 (KJV)

"He delighteth not in the strength of the horse, he taketh not pleasure in the legs of a man. The Lord taketh pleasure in them that fear him, in those that hope in his mercy. Praise the Lord O, Jerusalem; praise thy God O zion". Psalm 147:10-11 (KJV)

"For whosoever shall call upon the name of the Lord, shall be saved. How then shall thy call on him whom they have not believed? And how shall they believe in him, of whom they have not heard? And how shall they hear without a preacher? And how shall they preach except they be sent?" Romans 10:13-15 (KJV)

"Give and it shall be given unto you, good measure, pressed down, and shaken together and running over; shall men give into your bosom. For with the same measure that you mete withal, it shall be measured to you again". Luke 6:38 (KJV)

"Ye shall walk in all the ways which the Lord your God hath commanded you, that ye may live, and that it may be well with you, and that he may prolong your days in the land which ye shall possess". Deuteronomy 5:33 (KJV)

"I cried unto the thee, O Lord, I said, Thou art my refuge and my portion in the land of the living. Attend unto my cry, for I am brought very low, deliver me from my persecutors, for they are stronger than I". Psalm 142:5-6 (KJV)

"Rob not the poor, because he is poor, neither oppress the afflicted in the gate. For the Lord will plead their cause, and spoil the soul of those that spoiled them". Proverbs 22:22-23 (KJV)

There is a river whose streams shall make
Glad the City of God.
Psalm 46:4 (NKJV)

GROW IN HIS GRACE

You are God's special treasure
He has watched over you forever
You can slap his hands from holding you,
But never can his love not carry you through

His grace will help you grow
His mercies will follow wherever you go
Special Treasure you are to him,
Oh, praise the Lord, salvation He brings

He is King of all the earth,
A King has special treasures, He brings forth
You little princesses and prince so treasured,
Did you know His love for you, cannot be measured?

You are His segulah now and forever,
Sing for joy to the King and Savior
He made you special, oh, how marvelous
Enjoy your place of beauty He has made glorious!

Some Self Care For The Christian Women

1 Corinthians 6:19-20

Self Care is to unselfishly look after one's total body, mind and soul, spiritually, emotionally, and a mind set each day- before you or I can help others.

The Apostle Paul declares, "Be an example to others as I have been to you". "Follow me as I follow Christ." (1 Corinthians 11: 1-2)

Women saved or unsaved must not over indulge one's self and neglect others. We must not misuse our self care at the expense of being better than others because we can afford to do so and you cannot. Do not allow pride or selfish motives to cause others to stumble because of their lack of funds to do real self caring.

Self care is not only physical but very spiritual and healthy habits to keep practicing so we can help others to proper self caring. (1 Peter 3: 2-4) suggests that we self care not only physically, but spiritually, for there are other things to consider. Ie- a meek spirit, speaking kind words, graceful carriage, joyful, peaceful, pleasant, and being obedient as we walk to please the Lord.

Self caring takes in many attitudes and affirmed action.

1. Taking the time to look attractive

2. Cleansing of the whole body

3. Pleasant words to all people (Proverbs 25:11; 16:24)

4. Wearing your best smile and looking pleasant are good garments

5. Resting- know when to take a five and nourish your soul. Just chill.

6. Prayer time- nourish your spirit and pray for others

7. If you are married- let your husband leave the home with a picture of you that will make him want to hurry the day, and return home to you. So get out of the tatty robe and wear something lovely so that your smell and your self care will leave him with a spring in his step. This is no fooling-it works. hahahhaa.

THREE LADIES WHO I ADMIRED IN THEIR THEIR SELF CARE:

Esther- a future queen: She was self caring daily for about a year before she married the king. Bath oils, perfumes, hair care, lotions are all part of the care. She did it physically, emotionally as her attendant reassured her and spiritually in order to be a good help meet. What a future she looks forward to!

Lady Abigail: (1 Samuel 18) She was pleasant in behavior, speech, and general attitude to all the people around her including a very hostile and selfish husband. Nabal was not in his right frame of mind when he said unkind words about the future king David. The workers told her of the skillful way David and his men helped to save her family's livestock and how David was coming to kill all the men. She did a beautiful thing because she was a wise woman and she saved the day and a future king from bloodshed. Her deportment was noticed by the future king David who gave homage to her wisdom, charm, commonsense.I could even say, she practiced good physiology and conflict resolutions. I believed from that moment David had a desire for her to be part of his life. As soon as her evil hubby passed, he sent her a proposal and soon got married. Her self care in handling herself got David's eyes and heart. What a pay off? How is it with you single ladies, or widows?

Sarah: Oldest of the three women had her own beauty and rich self care. Noticed by her own husband, and then by a heathen king. One look at the graceful woman, he admired her and wanted her to be one of his Harem.-(Genesis 12:11-20) What a story? Age should never hinder good, proper self-care and preservation. May we learn from these women and others how they handle their own care physically, emotionally, financially and spiritually. They all work to make a better, confident and excellent woman (Proverbs 31). Note: Each of these dear women, would take up good time in your own personal studies.

SABATARGERS OF GOOD SELF CARING: (Ephesians 4: 17-32)

a. an angry personality, sour spirit, conceited and rude

b. Unforgiving, pouting, selfish women, lacking in understanding

c. Anxiousness, lack of peace and contentment, always thinking the worse

d. Getting over a painful hurt, critical spirit, self doubting, depression

e. e Guilt and forgiveness of self etc, etc.

BALANCING THE SCALE:

Do NOT neglect yourself even when you have to care for others- children, parents, friends, church and much more. Do something special for you. Have a good balance.

JESUS: He took time for himself- he was alone on the mountains talking with His Father- He took boat trips- enjoying his creation. He was tired on one of these boat trips and went to rest and napped . (Luke 8: 22-25). Jesus ate well with friends, He walked a lot so he got his exercise. He went to church (Synagogues) and He prayed an awful lot . How is your self caring and is it consistent? Follow His example.

YOU AND I MAINTAINING AND PRACTICING:

Let us continue and dress ourselves properly as we read in Colossians 4: 2-6) have an attitude of thankfulness, be a wise woman, don't try to build our house and then tear it down as a foolish woman would (Proverbs 14:1) Let us seize every opportunity to do the things that will make for better self care and help our younger women to do the same, honoring our God as His representative here on earth. Forgive yourselves, Take time out, be alone, make the time to re-examine and assess your motives, Asking for help when necessary. 'NO' can be a very sensible thing to say. Have a spa day, get a massage, read a good book, laugh and enjoy even laughing at yourself, (it is good medicine) enjoy your partner and do not make this intimate moment be like a curse or chore, and keep your heart from clutters.

"Beloved, I pray that you may prosper in all things
And be in health, just as your soul prospers".

3 John 1:2 (NKJV)

"Finding Intimacy with God in the Business of Life".

Luke 10: 38-42 (Amp). James 4: 8

INTIMACY (means closeness, warmth, nearness, familiarity, something special of a personal nature).

TAKING THE TIME (Mark 6:31) Come ye apart and rest...... Be refreshed, restored be well>

We are always busy with the general hassles of life; home, work, church, family, friends and sometimes even for ourselves. (commercial with the woman running back to her car and tried to take a five before facing her family),

There is a time and season for everything, says Ecclesiastes. 3- how or when or what we make time for- is the BIG question. Most times we get this nudge from the Holy Spirit to stop and come apart and spend some time with the Godhead but we delay the promptings, We make excuses, and sometimes we never obey and now it's time for bed. Wow! What now? This closeness is a two way affair- He always keeps His time with us- He never moves away but we do. Have you been MISSING your time with the Lord? What are you going to do about it now?

WOMEN IN THE BIBLE: It is said that there are 93 women mentioned- and we certainly can feel like some of them in our busy Martha's world.

Busy women come in many packages, Single, widowed, married, childless or have children. On a daily basis, we walk around with our checklist of to-do's- by the end of the day we have nothing left in the spiritual or emotional tank. Then later we face a partner who wants to be part of this closeness and you cringe. "Oh Lord, not now?" Haaaa. Our Lord was not able to give us the extra gas for the journey because we did not have this little nearness with Him during your day; – we were on our own like a butterfly flitting here and there. Beloved- we MUST meet Him in the morning for we certainly will NEED Him throughout the day! There were times when I had to go to the bathroom and cry out for help to satisfy my beloved intimately, and guess what, the God who make sex and all that goes with it HELPED me everytime I needed Him to be able to enjoy lovemaking and both of us are emotionally satisfied.

SOME BIBLICAL BUSY WOMEN:

1. Acts 16: 14 we have Lydia a Manufacturer and business savvy woman

2. Purple dye factory manager. Prayer and supporter of godly things.

3. Proverbs 31 Exceptional woman: Home maker, business, Commerce and Trade- family and community- even strangers. A spiritual woman.

4. Acts 18: Priscilla – a Tent maker, labor in trade with her hubby- and teacher of the word .Vs 18- she helped to disciple Apollos so he could refute the word rightly against agnosticism.

5. 1 Kings 16—Queen Jezebel--- Teacher, Organizer, had her finger on the pulse of her people and leaders of Baal. Her husband 's confidant.A no nonsense leader.

6. Luke 2 ---Anna – widowed and spiritual leader in her community and in the Temple, doing what was required of her especially as a Prayer Warrior.

7. Judges 4……Lawyer Deborah… Political,community, and savvy on Military power. She was spiritual and worked hard at it as a Judge in Israel.

God will NOT put more on us than we can do - but we do put a lot on our plate to our exhaustion. We NEED Time out so that we can have freshness and deeper affection for the things of the Lord. (Matthew 6:33) SEEK Him first, get to know Him and His ways more and more each week, month or year.

SOME PRINCIPLES IN BEING CLOSE AND INTIMATE WITH GOD:

a. First to know Him as Savior- washed in His Precious blood and have our sins forgiven. We cannot draw close to Him until we have come to know Him in this stage one. (Ephesians 2:1-9)

b. Prayer life has to be a must – we have a conversation with our Lord to know about his plans for you- and to let him know how he has changed you. (Psalm 5:3) "My voice you shall hear in the morning O Lord I have, for in the morning I will direct my prayer to you". Make the Lord your priority each day.

c. Knowing more about the new and lasting friendship with God: Reading His precious word. Once you've met the Master through Jesus at calvary-NOW you want to know more about him, and the future with him- Then READ His letter to you. It's PERSONAL- No one can be to you what He is or can be to YOU. (Ephesians 3: 16-18) You are loved daily by the Master, enjoy Him!

d. Worshipping Him- For all he has done in you, for you, and continues to do- Is precious. Our praise and thanks is to Him and He is glad when His child comes to Him with open heart of gratitude – needing nothing.

e. He should be our FIRST CHOICE- Make Him the top of your daily priority. He knows all things, and desires to impart them to you- He will keep his promises to you for He loves YOU and is concern about YOU."Walk worthy of God, who calls you into His own kingdom and glory. 1 Thessalonians 2:12 (NKJV).

A courtship will not last if the two people just merely and casually be together once in a while- This has to be maintained if it is going to get deeper even in marriage- Well, it is the same with getting to know God and all he has for each of us- It's a personal walk, It's a personal closeness, It's a personal choice to maintain this Intimacy, one hundred percent.

SOME WAYS TO RESTORE THIS CLOSENESS:

1. If you have small children or the plan of the day will be hectic- Get up half an hour or an hour before everyone and spend that time with the Lord.

2. At lunch time- go to your car- or find a place where you can seek Him if even for five or ten minutes- Get a fresh touch, grace and wisdom.

3. At the end of your day—ask for fresh grace to rekindle love between you and your spouse, and your children.(Susanna Wesley and her kids). She took the time with each one of them, and each got her attention, none were neglected.

4. Single and not dating- quiet your heart before Him in thanks, love, appreciation for keeping you all day- He took the time to protect and meet all your needs. He's worth some of your time, beloved, yes He does!

5. If You are home: put aside a certain time in the afternoon before your hubby gets home- and if he is at home- make time to freshen up yourself and make sure you are keeping your earthly relationship close as well as yours with God.

6. Share your heart about what the Lord is teaching you without finger pointing. Ask your husband to pray with you . It can be so much joy-as you grow and thrive with your Lord. We must make sure that Martha's business does NOT destroy or rob your closeness with people or with God. There is always tomorrow for work or other things.

Culture and time can change, but getting close to God should NOT change. There is power, strength, victory, and a vigor that will blow you away. Just try it for yourself and see the burst of growth you will have. You will be less critical, less gossipy, less complainer, less sour and more like your Lord day by day. (John 15:4 (NKJV) "Abide in me, and I in you as the branch cannot bear fruit, in itself unless it abides in the Vine neither can you, unless you abide in me".

How important is your closeness (Intimacy is to God? Closeness to your family, church, and how do you conduct your business in a busy Martha's world? You and I MUST remove all that hinders, that is distracting, weakening and making you feel guilty and stagnant.(Philippians 4:13. You can do it. Amen.

Begin with small changes and then as you get restored joy- stay vibrant and watch how the God who loves you will keep you glowing no matter life's test storms and trials. Philippians 4: 8-Think of lovely things, truthful, noble or honorable, Pure, and lovely or beautiful, and make for good reporting- if they are note-worthy, praiseworthy, let your mind reflect and meditate on them. Your heart will be strangely warmed by the fires of the Holy Spirit's power in you and others will see your growth as you live in a Martha's world. They will give praise to the Lord with you. Keep on growing in His grace in your busy world. Amen!

A TIME TO GIVE THANKS
A TIME TO GIVE PRAISE
A TIME TO CHANGE OUR UNGRATEFUL WAYS.

PSALM 95: 1-6

This Psalm begins with, 'O Come' it tells us that there is a reason to come. Why should we come? We come to sing, rejoice, give thanks, for He is our rock and salvation. That seems to be quite a lot to come and do. Yes, we have something to shout about, to give thanks for and to let our neighbors, friends, relations, everyone know that it is a GOOD thing to return thanks. Shout it out!

Our thanks is not just to someone but to the God of heaven and earth, for truly He has done some good things for you each day, each week, each month and every year you are on this good earth. Have you truly given Him your deepest appreciation for putting bread on your table, and protected you from all kinds of trauma and evils that is the norm of each day. God is displeased with our ungrateful attitude. However, He sends rain and blessings even when we are unthankful. What a gracious God to overlook our sins of ingratitude.We should repent of this sin and make the change.

We all learn to either be thankful or unthankful. In our homes from childhood, we learn bad habits too and how to treat folk even when they hurt us. I read about a lady who spoke about her Grandmother, how she taught her to deal with situations she herself faced by the hands of ungrateful and cruel friends. God does the same thing, forgiving us for our lack of appreciation to Him for all He does from morning till night everyday of our lives. Give Him thanks! The Bible records ungrateful Israel, complaining to Moses, Joshua, and all their leaders about what they needed, did not have or their own greed. They waited until they were being thrashed and rebuked, then they cried out, "God help us, God forgive us, God, we have sinned, God, we will change". They did change, but only for a short while and then a repeat of their sad story is recorded again and again. (Joshua chapter 24) Powerful words to Israel.

David the writer said, we should come with joyful singing, make joyful noises, come with your praises and tell the Lord God, El Shaddai, how grateful you are. Others, need to know about this God, who is above all other gods. You see, these so called gods have no power, they cannot speak, touch, give or do anything to deserve your praise- BUT, this God of heaven and earth and under the earth has everything- He is the source of life, He delights in us as His children, and always wants to bless us. Shout your thanks to Him now!

David goes on to say the very sea, and the dry land God made and they show their praises. Flowers bow their heads in praise-then why shouldn't you? (Verse 6), tells us that we are not humble enough to fall down before Him and pay homage for His kindnesses to you and yours. God loves when we are humble before Him; no pride and arrogance, for whatever you have He gave it to you or allowed you to get it. Remember, next time you and I think we made it on our own, to eat those words and turn to the God of heaven who had mercy on you and gave you what you do not deserve. His grace flows with mercy and love, and it's daily. Let Him know how grateful you are this day.

Psalm Chapter 96 : 4 (KJV) says, "For the Lord is great and greatly to be praised, he is to be feared above ALL gods". Verse 13 also reminds us that He is coming back again to judge the world with righteousness and truth". Make sure you lavish your praise now, for then it will be too late for some of you. The truth is, those who have embraced His free salvation, will be grateful and thankful daily, so that great day of judgment, they will only toss their Crowns and garlands of praise at His blessed feet. What will you have to greet Him, or what will you say then? Now is the time to practice and perform so on that day you will

be waiting hilariously to tell him how precious he has been to you and your family. As I write this, my heart is just bubbling over with joy- He helps me in sickness, in my financial lack, when I need wisdom, when I drive and I am not sure which way to go, how to deal with adult children, and so much more. He is always there, I just have to tap in His resources and praise Him for His Omnipotence.

The Apostle Paul reminded the Thessalonians to give thanks in ALL circumstances. This is not easy to do when we are chronic complainers- but try anyway. Most times when we pray we begin with a list of wants, right? Change the process instead of the 'give me' list, try to find even two things to begin your prayer of praise and thanks and you will find a sweeter joy in your prayer life.

Someone once said, we will grow like a string bean with stingy prayers, but when we praise and tell Father how thankful we are we grow like a robust plant. I am a farmer and there is not a time I am not thankful for the veggie growth and produce. I/we can sow but everything else comes through Him. Don't wait until November to be thankful, be thankful, appreciative and humble daily.

Most recently, I got an email from a family who are servants of the Lord, yet for two days they had no food- They were searching their hearts to see if anything in them was blocking the Lord's providing. They cried out for His divine intervention and hearts were touched to help with food and medical bills of his wife. I heard a song recently by the Brady group, "I have food on my table, shoes on my feet, God, I give you thanks for meeting my needs". Yes beloved, we are rich and prosperous more than we can ever think so each time you go to your Icebox, give thanks for the food in it- the bed you sleep on, good digestive system, a great mind, a country that is free for many to visit or live and so much more. Be a grateful person.

SPEAK THANKS TO OTHERS:

Make people feel nourishment in their soul by thanking them for the deeds of good they show to you and your family. Even a server at your store who has shown kindness to you, or a soldier who you meet somewhere, say, 'Thanks for your service'. I have seen their faces that they appreciate it, I am joyous when they say, "You are welcome Mam!". Bless someone today even if you think they do not deserve it- show mercy just like our Lord shows to you. In showing the world how to be thankful, we are showing them God and His love and blessings upon all the earth. I thank God for you who continue to read this and my other books. I thank Him for sending His precious Son to earth to die so that we can have salvation – free to us but costly to Him. He did it out of love for you, beloved.

It's my prayer that you are being blessed just as I was blessed writing this . I am always thankful as I write and very grateful to do it these many years. THANKS LORD FOR ALL YOUR BLESSINGS! Keep showering me and my friends and family with your special grace and we will forever be grateful for whatever you allow.

What do you have to be grateful for today, and how will you share His wonder and fantastic blessing? Don't hide your praise- He deserves it and others need to know how caring He is to all who come to Him.

Be thankful He's always very near
Be thankful all of your burdens He bears
Be thankful He's faithful to one and all
Be thankful he'll catch you if you fall.

Be thankful for the trials you are called to bear
Be thankful for the God who always hear
Be thankful that your trials will not last,
God is Lord over now, present and the past.

FISHING FOR ALL ETERNITY

Fishing is an art as we find the right bait for the various kinds of fish. Humankind is hardly any different- as it's never one size fits all- The Holy Spirit will teach us how to fish for men to help folk to see their need of a Savior and mend their ways by accepting Him the Lord Jesus as his or her own personal Lord and Savior.

No one is good enough to earn their salvation, we cannot give enough in the offering plate or bags, we cannot pray enough to enter heaven, Jesus told the man Nicodemus, "You must be born again". Nicodemus was a good man, served in the temple and other places of interest, but he was lost without Christ, so he went to have a talk with Jesus about his eternal salvation. Guess what? Nicodemus did. We read this story in the Book of John 3. What a change in this man? You can be changed also for now and all eternity. Will you, would you?.

FOLLOW ME: MARK 1:17 …. WHY SHOULD WE FOLLOW?
BECOMING A BUSINESSMAN /WOMAN FOR THE SOULS OF FOLK.
SIN: THE CAUSE…..CHRIST IS THE ONLY CURE (Romans 6:23)

AN UNREPENTANT HEART IF NOT CHANGED WILL BE SENTENCED TO A CHRISTLESS ETERNITY AND TOTAL SEPARATION FOREVER FROM GOD. The story in Luke sixteen verse nineteen to thirty one, is very important for it sets the stage now to make sure we know where we will be in eternity. Where will you be, which side will you be on? Don't wait too long, time is running out.

JESUS: HIS HOME
HIS PERSON
HIS MESSAGE
HIS PURPOSE………………IT SHOULD BE OURS TOO EVEN IN WEAKNESS
FISHERMEN: THE PEOPLE
THE CALLED
THE MESSAGE
THE PROMISE
THE CALL TO FOLLOW CONTINUES

WE FOLLOW WITHOUT RESERVATION, DEALS, DEBATES OR REASONING- TOTALLY WILLING? MAYBE NOT! WHEN WE SURRENDER, IT BRINGS JOY AND DEPENDENCE ON THE HOLY SPIRIT'S HELP.

-IT'S A PARTNERSHIP WITH CHRIST- WE ARE NOT DOING IT ALONE- "I WILL MAKE you Fishers of men". Observe others and their fishing strategies and find your way- timid or not.

- **The PLAN:** make the message simple- use a few verses to make your statements. Mark your bible so you know how to get to it.

-**THE MESSAGE:** Make your message clear, ie like a company logo and Policy- Share your testimony of your Turn Around, when it happened or even where you were then.

- **YOUR PRAYER:** Water your days with prayer as the Lord sends someone to your door or along your path. Take their prayer request- PRAY for them right then if possible.

- **THE ETERNAL REWARDS:** Now and in the future is assured. (John 14) He has gone to secure a special Place for all those who will repent and make Him Lord of their lives now on earth. Jesus paid the ultimate price for our sins for we are all born sinners because of our first parent's disobedience. "All have sinned and fall short of ever becoming sinless." Romans 3:23 declared this. We all must come humbly before the Lord Jesus and ask for His forgiveness and take care of this fact before you leave this earth, for there is NO repentance in the grave says the Lord Jesus. Do it now and you will be glad you did- even when the storms of life hit hard, you can still have and enjoy His peace each and every day. He will help you to thrive and bloom for His glory and praise.

Isaiah 55:1-3; 6 -7 says we are to come and yield your heart to Him Amen.

A DESPERATE CRY FOR HELP

In our world today, there is always a cry bellowing out- Someone is always calling for help – some more desperate than others never-the-less we can hear it and how we respond is another matter. "When I call, He will answer". He is the Lord Jesus, who is always listening for the one who will cry or the one crying for help; they hope they will touch his ears and he will respond. (Isaiah 65:24)

There are many types of cries for help- I don't know your cry- What is it?

* A cry of joy, something fantastic has happened hence the joyful cry.

* A Mournful cry- because of a death, a sadness, bad news, pain or accidents

* A cry because of hunger and the need for food, water or something to alleviate such desperate need to live or quench the thirst.

* A cry because an individual is being raped, or about to be murdered or beaten

What is Your Cry?

What is your cry, desperate, or not as dramatic- but you know you are in trouble and really need someone to rescue you- You hope they will hear your cry, silently, or an outburst to wake up someone to rush to their aid.

On a Monday morning in August, 2018, I heard a cry for help that moved my heart which caused me to investigate where the sound was coming from. It was the cry of a baby kitten alone and in the cool morning mist by the side of my house. "Oh, boy", I said- You see, her mother Decker, had four babies and after many days Decker removed three of the kittens and left this little, not –so-strong one and there she was all alone, no mother, no milk, no siblings and no comfort from the family. Wow! This is a serious cry and what must I do now?

Can you think back of a time when you were frightened because you were alone or felt alone, abandoned, and fearful and needed help? Yea, I have had some of those times in my life and I had to call on Jesus the Savior of the world for help to rescue me from the danger I felt. Glory to Him, he did hear my cry and yes, He delivered me. Our brother Jonah, cried from the depths of the sea as he was in the belly of the great fish and our Lord heard his cry of repentance. (Jonah 2: 2) There is never a doubt when we call the God of the universe for His help and he does not respond. He watches day and night with love and compassion. (Psalm 69: 16)

TINKERBELL is the name I gave her- her eyes are not open as yet but she is a fighter and makes no bone about crying for help. My girlfriend went, and bought us a baby nipple bottle and various nipples and a can of milk. We went to work, and tried to feed Tinkerbell, and yes, she sucked on the nipple and got a good drink and then went to sleep- You cannot believe what was going on trying to help this frightened, abandoned baby kitten. Decker, her mother, has not returned so I am the new mother feeding her three times a day, and making sure she has a bottle with warm water, thinking her warm mommy is beside her. Oh my, the things we do for love, care, and response to a cry!

PEOPLE OR ANIMALS?

Many folk care about their animals more than caring for people and the other side is also true, more about people and less about animals. There can and should be a balance. People run the world, not animals. We love animals, but there should be even more care to humans for humans can respond in many ways an animal can't. Humans have to make choices between heaven or hell eternally- animals don't and cannot. Folk have had the cart before the horse because of some trauma they encountered in their lifetime- however, there is a place for animals but never at the cost of a human child or adult.

Jesus Christ the Savior of the world died for humans not for animals and even with love the two are not compatible and should never be misplaced in the line of purpose now and in the life to come. People die and leave millions of dollars for their animals, while family members, or many others they knew before they died, are crying out for help and deliverance and they have not responded to their cries. It's a shame to stop listening to human cries and abandonment and sufferings. Money can support both causes- and make many folk happy. Including the dying as they share their money to help people and animals.

My Tinkerbell will be nursed until she is stronger and then I will take her to the local shelter for adoption. I have counted the cost of having an animal or a child, but I am not able to have any living with me- for one, I have very little fund to do this, and secondly, I am allergic to cats among other things. A child takes care, cost, time and almost every energy to give the proper care she or he will need. Knowing one's limitations is key- I can help my neighborhood cats and then do the better thing by taking them to the shelter to get into a home where someone can help make her life better, and they both will have a joyful relationship for a very long time.

ADOPTION: This is a cry we hear all the time, on radio, or the Telly about children who need a good home and sometimes the children say what they are hoping for if and when they are adopted. Their heart is crying out for desperate help and when things have not worked out they get depressed, angry and the feeling of being abandoned by society. I believe that people want to adopt someone or something, but after they have counted the cost, they have to say no and they do have that right instead of saying yes and later find out it is out of their reach. God bless those who are able, and if you are, do not discount those of us who are not able at this time. Pray and care as you are able and know this that you will be appreciated for what you can or cannot do.

SALUTE TO ALL:

Whatever you do either to adopt a human or animal do it because you are able without grudge, biases, and complaining. We will respect you if you try and fail and there is no shame. No one can tell your circumstances but you . Make sure you think it through and pray concerning your choices- and show both love, care, and understanding. If you cannot keep the adopted thing you choose to have, then share in the upkeep if you can. Many folk are able to give something to help in the care of animals or humans. Just be giving for the sake of love, caring and giving towards future happiness and joy. Blessing on whatever your decision will be in helping to make our world a better place, a happy place, joyful place, and a loving place.

NOTE: Remember to buy my books for children- Mr Whiskers, and "The Cats Who Adopted Me" .

LIVING THROUGH TOUGH AND STORMY TIMES

These days, we hear and read the news of the "Me Too" movement-

No matter what we think as we listen or read, many women are still traumatized by tough and rough times in their abusive, unkind, and undervalued situations. Yes, life can be tough, painful and for some they think they have reason to do damage to their life, because they feel hopeless and dejected- they wonder will my life change for the better? God help me/us!

Each week I will hear stories of women in my community of their stormy and tough times as they make the best of living situations. Some are living in fear, some are like the Woman at the Well, waiting for a Savior to come and rescue them and their children. I can either ignore or give my sympathy and pray with them for an answer or just feel sorry for them and pass by. How would you handle these tough stormy times so many are facing at this time of their lives.

Bible Women: Most if not all these precious women had different challenges in living in tough and difficult times. I think of Hagar in Genesis 21, she was kicked out of her home with a child to take care of alone. Abraham, the father of the boy, just sent her away without any support- only with a bottle of water and some bread- Tell me, how far would that take them? As they cried out for help to the God of Abraham –El Roi He heard, He saw and He delivered care that was lacking- God gave her water, comfort and a promise of blessing WOW! How is this in a time of stress and hard time and even death in a very hot desert in the days and very cold nights. Hallelujah for divine help in our hard times and stormy times of abandonment.

(2) What about Abigail in and her cruel husband Nabal who was so abusive and unkind everyone knew about his behavior. This sister did what was good and all the workers could see her under pressure. God also delivered her too. Her good and wise counsel to the future king David and she became his wife after the death of Nabal her curlish husband. Now, delivered from her pain and sorrows. (1 Samuel 25) He can do the same for you too, no matter the tough times or stormy times you are experiencing.

One day last week a lady called the church phone seeking help to get out of her tough situation with her two teenagers. Abused, forsaken, by her live-in partner- no place to go, and pure confusion. I began at the beginning, -Her spiritual condition- and moved from there. I tried to bring hope and joy knowing that she is loved by the Greatest man, Jesus the Christ who has been rescuing women from when He was on earth to this very day. Dear Reader, most times the spiritual condition of a heart is more than the actual tough times we face. When we take the first step of the spiritual, most times other things become clearer to the Seeker and other things fall in place, because Jesus does NOT leave us in our dire state He makes a way amen! Isaiah 41:10 is still true today. Just believe Him for every challenge.

Single women have tougher times, widows too, and young girls. The Little Maid (servant teen girl) taken from her home, friends and family to a strange and far-away land is a prime example of tough time adjusting to her new homeland. (2 Kings 5) Can you even imagine this if you were in her shoes, like those today who have had to leave home because of world wars and intimidation and even death for some, because they follow Jesus the Christ?. I remembered when I came to Wisconsin to attend New Tribes Missions Mission school-I was Cold, confused as to why I was here, thin tropical clothes, I was in need of winter clothes and a new attitude of this change in weather for many months. Adjustment was the need of the hour- What should I do, where could I get winter clothes without money? God opened the hearts of a couple to adopt me and bought all I would be needing for that and many more winters. Praise be to the Lord! He did hear my silent cries for health, and clothing. I needed a friend who could understand the agony I was sifting through and the cost for these things.

This exceptional Teen did not allow her new life to block her perception of those who needed God's help- and so she reached out to Mrs. Naaman about her leprous husband, although Naaman was snobbish and did not want to be healed the way things were set up, he humbled himself and dipped in the Jordan river seven times as was the command. God took over and he was healed- Just supposed she spent her time bemoaning her tough times thinking of her life, what do you think would have happened to Mr. Naaman? These stories God is telling in the Bible His word, are for us to take heart, for what is happening to us is not new, others have gone before us and the same help they got we can too for Jehovah God is for all times, and seasons. Chin up Pilgrims we are heading for better times, Amen!

"God shall wipe away all tears from our eyes and there shall be no more death Neither sorrows or crying, neither any more pain for the former things are have passed away". Revelations 21: 4-6).

HERE ARE SOME THINGS TO THINK AND MEWS ON: (I did this at a Women's conference a few years ago).

1. What was one of the toughest times you went through and how did you get through it?

2. How have you benefited from going through tough times—How?

3. Since tough times can be (a) my own making (b) caused by others (c) permitted by the Lord- Which category are you in or have been in?

4. If you could turn back the hand of time, how would you avoid tough and stormy times or could you?

5. Can a believer grow up without going through tough times- is it necessary?

6. Which Scripture or story helped you in your tough and stormy times? Share and bless others

7. Have you been angry or resentful in your tough times?...Why

8. Have you been able to help others because of your victories?

Repenting, Rebooting, Renewing rejoicing and Testifying

It does not matter what times we face, Our loving, healing, kind, and gracious God is there to hear us- Now, He may deliver pronto or we will have to wait for whatever He is trying to make of us – it's up to Him for the time for our deliverance. I plead with you, just watch, and with joyful heart expect His answer. Our tough and stormy times are only temporary, and we are never alone as we go through. When He answers, remember to use this platform to testify of His blessings, and help others in their time of weeping, anxiousness, and doubts to hold on . "His answer is on the way- Do you remember the story of the woman who expected rain in a time of drought and took her umbrella and galoshes to the evening meeting at her church- when others laughed at her, guess what? The rain came and she was the only one ready for it. The laugh was on them.

Expect our Lord to work, doubting is unbelief and our God wants you and me to BELIEVE Him at all times. This faith honors Him and brings joy to His heart. Are you ready for His blessing in your tough and stormy times? Then act like you are expecting a bucketful of blessing and a turn-about of our tough times (Psalm 27:13-14).

Dance as if no one is looking, and sing of His praises because you are expecting an answer from the God Who hears and delivers according to our needs. Look up child, it won't be long now, wash your face and fix up your heart for the rejoicing of your deliverance, and sing His praises of how He helped you to cross over these tough and stormy times you have faced, will face or is facing. " He is our portion and refuge in the land of the living" Psalm 142: 4-5) This too will pass beloved- Hope in your God!

Carmen was accredited (ordained) as a minister of the gospel many years ago by Bethany Bible Chapel in Kingston, Jamaica, and Germantown Christian Assembly, Pennsylvania. She has been involved with ministries at the Willingboro Christian Assembly and Applied Bible Concepts ministries in New Jersey for thirty years. She is a much sought after Minister of the Gospel, Motivational Speaker, Workshop leader, Trained in Healthcare Services, Children Story Teller, and Authors six books, and eleven gospel leaflets being used all over the world.

Since 2009 Carmen has written articles for the Lilies of the Field Bi-monthly Magazine; Online Blogger, and much more. She's kept busy as she encourages women, Girls and men, making sure they are enjoying their lives and being the best they can be regardless of what life storms they are facing.

Carmen has two grown children and three grandchildren. You can find her books where books are sold and you will be supporting evangelism, missions and general care to all people.

Carmen's life partner Ed, made a good team with fantastic ministry until his death . Their family are very supportive and are serving the Lord in their own way of directives.

AWARDS AND HONORS:

October, 2006   Carmen was honored and work acknowledged in Missions at home and abroad, by her church's Mission's Department, Willingboro Christian Assembly, New Jersey.

April, 2014   Midland Bible Institute, Jamaica, W.I, honored her for her contribution to this Institution, her inspirational, motivational and financial contribution in helping to make this fine school a blessing to all.

May, 2014   The Willingboro Christian Ladies Fellowship, honored Carmen for Tireless work among them since 1987 and to the Community at large, Making the community a place of blessing, safety and peace.

October, 2014   Carmen was one of the many recipients who received President Obama's Presidential Award for her National and Local Community Services.

I give all the praise to the Lord who called me to serve His cause many years ago. Thanks for your kind and gracious help in making service to the King of Kings a pleasure.

Carmen is open for your calls to speak and help motivate God's people in taking up the cross as a good soldier and march on forward sharing His love for all people.

Email – charmingandy1@gmail.com, call – 609-871-4011. cel 267 594 2801

Printed in the United States
by Baker & Taylor Publisher Services